GODS and GODDESSES
of ~Ancient Greece~

by Danielle Smith-Llera

raintree
a Capstone company — publishers for children

Raintree is an imprint of Capstone Global Library Limited, a company incorporated in England and Wales having its registered office at 264 Banbury Road, Oxford, OX2 7DY – Registered company number: 6695582

www.raintree.co.uk
myorders@raintree.co.uk

Edited by Aaron Sautter
Designed by Bobbie Nuytten
Picture research by Svetlana Zhurkin
Production by Jennifer Walker

ISBN 978 1 4747 1746 5
19 18 17 16 15
10 9 8 7 6 5 4 3 2 1

British Library Cataloguing in Publication Data
A full catalogue record for this book is available from the British Library.

Photo Credits

Alamy: bilwissedition Ltd. & Co. KG, 20, dieKleinert, 7; Newscom: Album/Joseph Martin, 13, Universal Images Group/Leemage, 18; Shutterstock: abxyz, 6, Anastasios71, cover (right), 1, andersphoto, 19, Artishok, 21 (back), Cyril Hou, cover (left), 16, Danilo Ascione, 17, Dimitrios, 14, Ensuper (paper), back cover (top) and throughout, ilolab (grunge background), cover, 1, Kamira, back cover (bottom right), 15 (front), Maxim Kostenko (background), 2 and throughout, mexrix, 5 (back), 15 (back), PerseoMedusa, 9, Roberto Castillo (column), back cover and throughout, Sergey Goryachev, 8, Thorsten Rust, 10; SuperStock: DeAgostini, 12, Fine Art Images, 11; XNR Productions, 5 (map)

We would like to thank Jonathan M. Hall, professor at the University of Chicago, for his invaluable help in the preparation of this book.

CONTENTS

WATCHING FROM THE MOUNTAIN

The ancient Greeks honoured and worshiped several gods and goddesses. They believed the gods watched over people from their home on Mount Olympus. The Greeks thought the gods controlled things, such as earthquakes, the weather and when people died. Today, we know Greek gods were just **myths**. Let's look at the family of Greek gods and what people once believed about them.

myth story told by people in ancient times; myths often tried to explain natural events

4

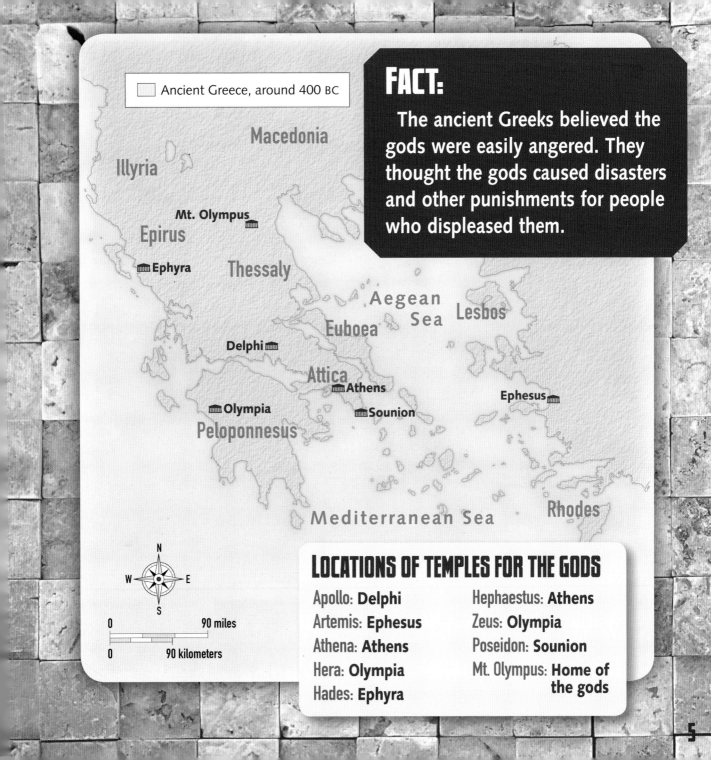

Ancient Greece, around 400 BC

Macedonia

Illyria

Epirus

Mt. Olympus

Ephyra

Thessaly

Aegean Sea

Lesbos

Euboea

Delphi

Attica

Athens

Ephesus

Olympia

Sounion

Peloponnesus

Mediterranean Sea

Rhodes

N
W — E
S

0   90 miles

0   90 kilometers

FACT:

The ancient Greeks believed the gods were easily angered. They thought the gods caused disasters and other punishments for people who displeased them.

LOCATIONS OF TEMPLES FOR THE GODS

Apollo: **Delphi**

Artemis: **Ephesus**

Athena: **Athens**

Hera: **Olympia**

Hades: **Ephyra**

Hephaestus: **Athens**

Zeus: **Olympia**

Poseidon: **Sounion**

Mt. Olympus: **Home of the gods**

ZEUS

Zeus was the king of the sky and all the Greek gods. The ancient Greeks believed Zeus controlled the weather. They also thought Zeus had a bad temper. When he was displeased, he hurled thunderbolts at those who angered him. However, stories also show that Zeus tried to rule fairly and shared power with his family.

FACT:

One story about Zeus tells of Typhon, a fierce monster with 100 serpent heads. When Typhon attacked Mount Olympus, all the other gods fled. But Zeus defeated him by picking up Mount Aetna and burying Typhon underneath it.

A huge statue of Zeus was considered one of the wonders of the ancient world.

HERA

Hera was Zeus' wife and the goddess of marriage. But Zeus often fell in love with human women. Zeus had a son, Heracles, with a human woman. This made Hera **jealous** and angry. When Heracles was a baby, Hera sent snakes to try to kill him.

jealous want something someone else has

ruins of a temple to Hera in Italy

POSEIDON

Zeus' brother, Poseidon, ruled the seas. Greeks trembled at his changing moods. With his **trident**, Poseidon could make the earth quake and the seas rise. The Greeks believed floods were Poseidon's punishment for those who displeased him. When the seas were calm, sailors believed Poseidon was content.

trident long spear with three sharp points at the end

FACT:

According to myth, Poseidon created the horse and gave it as a gift to humans. The Greeks believed a galloping horse moved like the ocean's waves.

HADES

Greeks feared meeting Hades, the god of the dead. Even Hades' brother, Zeus, avoided him. The Greeks believed that Hades punished people who disrespected the gods. Hades' three-headed dog, Cerberus, is found in several Greek myths. Cerberus guarded the entrance to the **Underworld** and kept the dead from escaping.

Underworld place under the earth where ancient Greeks believed the spirits of the dead went

HADES AND SISYPHUS

In one story, a king named Sisyphus used several tricks to escape death. But Hades finally captured him. As punishment for his tricks, Hades forced Sisyphus to push a boulder up a steep hill. But it always rolled back down. Sisyphus was forced to repeat his punishment forever.

ATHENA

Zeus' favourite child, Athena, was the goddess of wisdom. She often helped people. Athena gave Perseus a special shield, which he used to defeat the snake-haired monster, Medusa. But Athena could also be **spiteful**. In one myth, a woman claimed to weave more beautifully than Athena. The goddess punished the woman by turning her into a spider.

spiteful desire to hurt, annoy or offend someone

ATHENA: CRAFTSMEN'S FRIEND

Athena was also the goddess of crafts. The Greeks believed Athena invented the potter's wheel. The Greeks used potter's wheels to make clay pots, which held wine as an offering to the gods. They often painted these pots with characters and events from Greek myths.

ARTEMIS

Artemis was the goddess of hunting. She enjoyed life in the forest with her bow and silver arrows. This daughter of Zeus never married. She preferred hunting with female friends. The Greeks believed Artemis protected children. She also watched over young women until they married.

FACT:

One Greek myth says that a hunter once spied on Artemis as she bathed in a lake. Artemis became very angry and turned him into a deer. His own hunting dogs then killed him.

a sculpture of the hunter who was punished by Artemis, in Caserta, Italy

APOLLO

Artemis' handsome twin brother, Apollo, was Zeus' favourite son. This proud god of music loved playing his stringed **lyre**. Apollo had a short temper. One story says he once gave donkey ears to a king who disliked his music. But Apollo was also generous. The Greeks believed that he allowed visitors to see their own futures at his temple in Delphi.

APOLLO IN LOVE

One myth tells of how Apollo fell in love with a **nymph** named Daphne. When he chased after her, she turned into a laurel tree to escape him. But Apollo still loved Daphne. So he took care of the laurel tree and claimed it as his symbol. The Greeks often used laurel leaves to crown leaders and winners of competitions.

lyre small, stringed, harplike instrument
nymph beautiful, female spirit or goddess who lived on a mountain, in a forest or in a body of water

HEPHAESTUS

Hephaestus walked with a limp and relied on a walking stick. The Greeks believed his mother, Hera, threw him off Mount Olympus because he was so ugly. Inside a volcano, Hephaestus learnt to be a **blacksmith**. He created powerful weapons and armour, such as Zeus' thunderbolts and Athena's shield. Hephaestus later returned to Mount Olympus as the god of metalwork and fire.

blacksmith someone who makes and fixes metal objects

Family tree of the gods

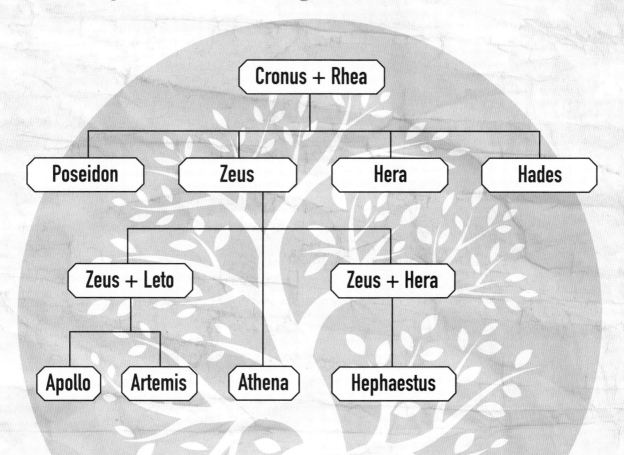

Cronus + Rhea

Poseidon | Zeus | Hera | Hades

Zeus + Leto | Zeus + Hera

Apollo | Artemis | Athena | Hephaestus

The Greek gods and goddesses were all part of one big family. Like human families, they were all related to one another as brothers, sisters, aunts, uncles and cousins.

Glossary

blacksmith someone who makes and fixes metal objects

jealous want something someone else has

lyre small, stringed, harplike instrument

myth story told by people in ancient times; myths often tried to explain natural events

nymph beautiful, female spirit or goddess who lived on a mountain, in a forest or in a body of water

spiteful desire to hurt, annoy or offend someone

trident long spear with three sharp points at the end

Underworld place under the earth where ancient Greeks believed the spirits of the dead went

Read more

Ancient Greeks (Beginners), Stephanie Turnball (Usborne Publishing Ltd, 2015)

Greek Myths and Legends (All About Myths), Jilly Hunt (Raintree, 2013)

You Wouldn't Want to be a Slave in Ancient Greece!: A Life You'd Rather Not Have (You Wouldn't Want To), Fiona Macdonald (Franklin Watts, 2014)

Websites

www.ancientgreece.co.uk
Learn all about ancient Greece on The British Museum website.

www.bbc.co.uk/history/anicent/greeks/
Explore topics about the ancient Greeks, such as the Olympic Games, theatres and gods.

Comprehension questions

1. In your own words, explain why the ancient Greeks believed that the gods controlled everything that happened in the world.

2. Look at the Family Tree of the Gods on page 21. How were Zeus, Poseidon and Hades related to each other?

Index